King Sejong's Gift

Seong min Yoo

Text copyright © 2025
Illustration copyright © 2025

All rights reserved. No part of this publication may be reproduced or transmitted in any form or by any means, electronic or mechanical, including photocopying, recording or by any information storage and retrieval system now known or to be invented, without permission in writing from the publisher.

Layout and design by Seong min Yoo
ISBN 978-1-0693151-7-5

Able Beaver Press Co. fuels creativity and continues to publish books for every reader. Thank you for buying an authorized edition of this book. The artwork in this book was rendered in watercolour and gouache.

Written and illustrated by Seong min Yoo
Proofing by Scott MacKenzie

2 4 6 8 10 9 7 5 3

For all those who find joy in every new word

Emily likes Korean music. She enjoys the melody but not so much the lyrics. Mom asks one day, "Emily, do you know what those songs are about?" "No, but they would be more enjoyable if I understand them." Emily answers.

에밀리는 한국음악을 좋아해요. 멜로디는 즐겁게 듣지만 가사는 그렇지 않죠. 어느날 엄마가 에밀리에게 "그 노래가 무엇인지 알겠니?" 라고 물어 보아요. "아니요, 하지만 그것들을 이해 한다면 더 즐거울 것 같아요." 에밀리가 대답해요.

"Can you guess by any chance who made the Korean alphabet?" Mom asks. "Well, Hmmm, I'm not sure." She replies. "It was created by King Sejong the Great of the Joseon Dynasty in 1443." Mom says. "Oh, I see!" Emily exclaims.

"혹시 한국어 알파벳을 만든 사람이 누구인지 맞춰 볼 수 있겠니?" 엄마가 물어요. "글쎄요, 잘 모르겠어요." 에밀리가 대답해요. "그것은 1443년 조선의 세종대왕에 의해 창제 되었단다." 엄마가 말해요. "아, 그렇구나!" 에밀리가 외쳐요.

"The literacy rate was not very high at that time among commoners as the written Chinese characters were used only by the upper class. It was a different form to the spoken language and was restricted as it was so difficult for ordinary citizens to learn. So they were having trouble expressing their thoughts or communicating on a daily basis."

"그 당시 중국어 문자는 상류층만 사용해서 평민들의 문해율은 그리 높지 않았지. 구어체 언어와 형태가 달랐고 일반 시민들이 배우기에는 너무 어려웠기 때문에 제한적이었어. 그래서 그들은 자신들의 생각을 표현하거나 소통하는데 매일 어려움을 겪고 있었지."

Mom continues. "King Sejong, who loved his people and felt sorry for the struggles that they had faced, wanted to help them get the proper education they deserved." "Oh, so what happened to them?" Emily asks.

엄마가 계속 말씀하세요. "백성들을 사랑했고 그들이 겪었던 고충을 안타까워 했던 세종대왕은 그들이 마땅히 받아야 할 교육을 받을 수 있도록 돕고 싶어 하셨단다." "아, 그래서 어떻게 되었어요?" 에밀리가 물어봐요.

"King Sejong published Hunminjeongeum which is the original name of the Korean alphabet, it means the right sounds to teach the people, and it explained the logic and science behind it.

"세종대왕은 한국어 문자의 원래 이름인 훈민정음을 출간 하셨는데, 그것은 사람들을 가르치기 위한 올바른 소리를 의미하며, 논리와 과학을 설명하는 내용 또한 담고 있지.

ㄱ ㄴ ㄷ ㄹ ㅁ ㅂ ㅅ
ㅇ ㅈ ㅊ ㅋ ㅌ ㅍ ㅎ

ㅏ ㅑ ㅓ ㅕ ㅗ ㅛ ㅜ
ㅠ ㅡ ㅣ

It is remarkably easy to learn, with its own unique sounds, separate from Chinese characters, consisting of 28 letters of 17 consonants and 11 vowels, but 4 gradually disappeared, leading to the current 24 letters." She explains.

그것만의 고유한 소리를 가진, 한자와 구분된, 배우기가 놀라울 정도로 쉬운 훈민정음은 17개의 자음과 11개의 모음인 28자로 이루어져 있었지만 점차 4개가 사라져서 현재의 24개가 되었단다." 엄마가 설명해요.

"Later on in 1912, the name of Hangeul was coined by Korean linguist Ju Si-gyeong. Han means great and geul means script." Mom cites.

"그 후 1912년에 언어학자 주시경에 의해 한글 이라는 이름이 만들어졌단다. '한'은 위대한 것을 의미하고 '글'은 문자를 의미해." 엄마가 말해요.

"Hangeul is one of the most logically designed phonetic alphabets in the world creating more than 11,000 different syllable blocks." Mom says. "Oh, wow, that is beyond my imagination." Emily is amazed. "Yes, it is, isn't it?" Mom smiles. "I wonder what Hangeul looks like and how it is written." Emily is curious.

"한글은 세계에서 가장 논리적으로 만들어진 음성문자들 중에 하나로 11,000개 이상의 다양한 음절 블록을 만들어 내지." 엄마가 말해요. "와~ 상상을 초월 하네요." 에밀리가 놀라워 해요. "그래, 그렇지 않니?" 엄마가 미소 지어요. "한글이 어떻게 생겼는지, 어떻게 쓰여지는지 궁금해요." 에밀리가 알고 싶어하죠.

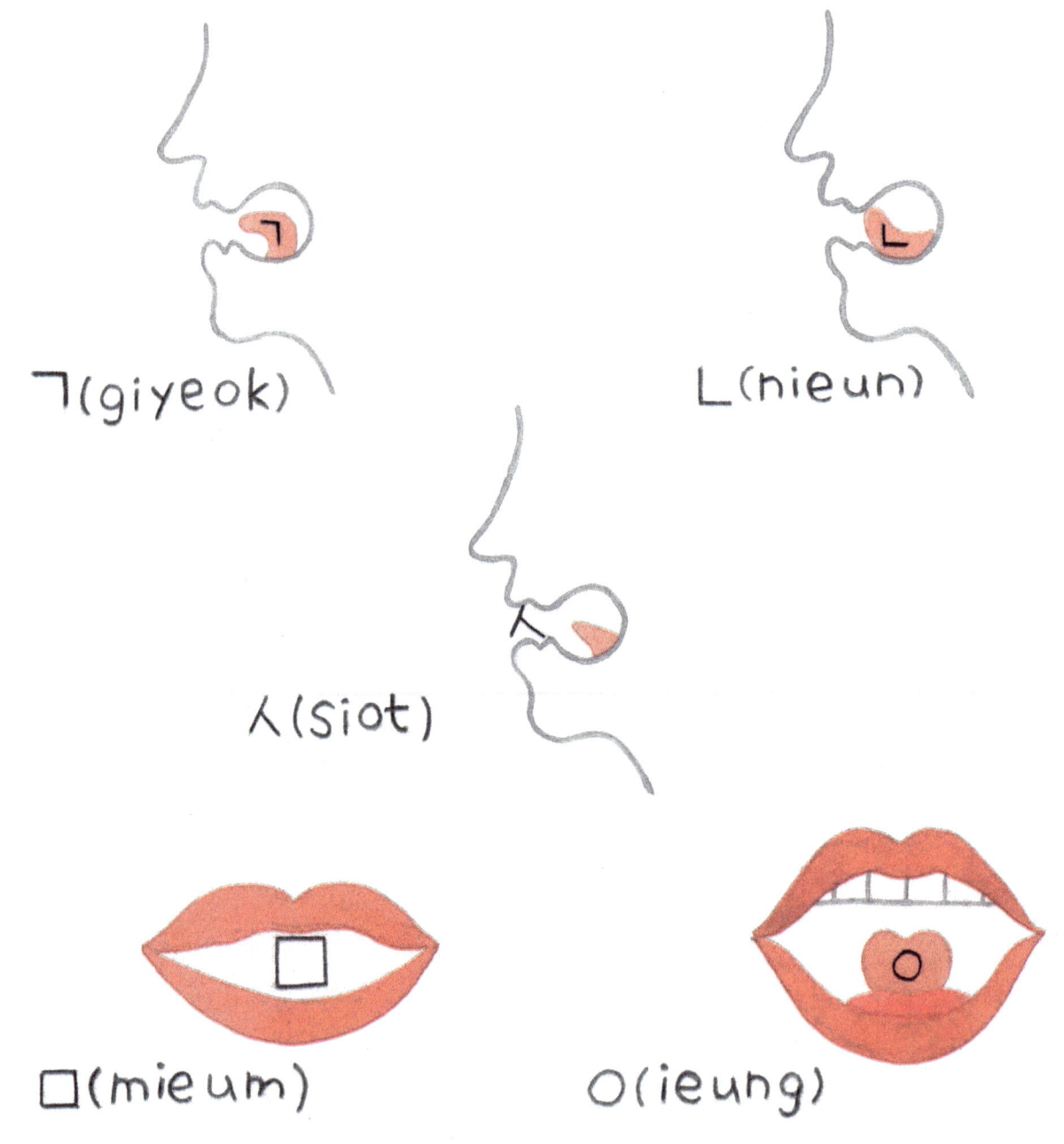

"Here they are, the five basic consonants are ㄱ(g) ㄴ(n) ㅁ(m) ㅅ(s) ㅇ(ng)" Mom points out. "These are so fascinating." Emily shouts with joy. Mom mentions that Korean consonants are a sound that comes from the back of the tongue or throat like ㄱ ㅇ, a sound made using the front part of the tongue like ㄴ ㅅ and a sound of two lips touching like ㅁ.

"여기 다섯 개의 기본 자음으로 ㄱ,ㄴ,ㅁ,ㅅ,ㅇ이 있단다." 엄마가 알려주어요. "정말 흥미로운 걸요." 에밀리가 기뻐서 소리쳐요. 이 자음들은 혀의 뒤쪽이나 목구멍에서 나는 소리 ㄱ ㅇ, 혀의 앞 부분을 사용해서 내는 소리 ㄴ ㅅ 그리고 두 입술이 닿아 나는 소리 ㅁ이 있다고 엄마가 이야기 해요.

Emily tries to imitate the sound. She pronounces giyeok triumphantly. "Yes, you are really good." Mom says. She tells Emily that more letters can be created by adding strokes of one or two to the basic consonants. ㅋ-k(kieuk) ㄷ-d(digeut) ㅌ-t(tieut) ㄹ-r(rieul) ㅂ-b(bieup) ㅍ-p(pieup) ㅈ-j(jieut) ㅊ-ch(chieut) ㅎ-h(hieut)

에밀리가 소리를 따라 하려고 해요. 에밀리는 자신있게 기역 이라고 발음해요. "정말 잘 하네." 엄마가 말해요. 기본 자음에 1~2개의 획을 추가하면 더 많은 글자를 만들 수 있다고 엄마가 에밀리에게 이야기 해요. 키읔, 디귿, 티읕, 리을, 비읍, 피읖, 지읒, 치읓, 히읗

Sky

Person

Earth

Basic Vowels

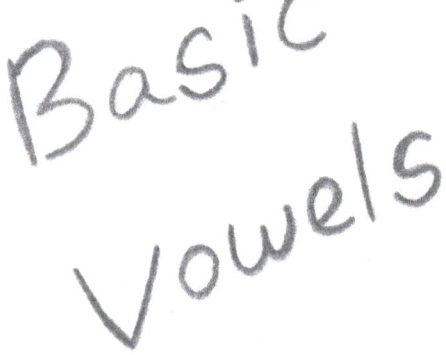

"Hangeul is very fun to learn. What about vowels, how are they made and how do they look?" Emily couldn't wait to discover more. "The basic vowels were made out of three elements and they were derived from the shapes representing heaven, earth and human. • represented the roundness of the sky, — represented the flat earth and ǀ symbolized a person who was standing between the sky and the earth."

"한글 배우는 게 정말 재미있어요. 모음은 어때요, 그것들은 어떻게 만들어졌고 모양은 어떤가요?" 에밀리는 더 많은 것들을 알고 싶어 해요. "기본 모음은 세 가지 요소로 구성되어 있으며 하늘, 땅 그리고 인간을 나타내는 형태에서 유래 되었지. • 는 하늘의 둥글림을 나타냈고, — 는 평평한 지구를 표현했으며 ǀ 는 하늘과 땅 사이에 서 있는 사람을 상징했단다."

"Oh, what did they sound like then?" Emily asks. "The sky symbol represented a sound similar to Ah, the earth was similar to Eu, the person was similar to Ee. King Sejong applied this oriental philosophy to embody the harmonization between all 3 elements, developing more vowels." Mom says.

"아, 그럼 그것들은 어떻게 소리가 났죠?" 에밀리가 물어요. "하늘의 상징은 '아'와 비슷한 소리를 나타냈고, 땅은 '으'로, 사람은 '이'와 비슷하게 발음했지. 세종대왕은 이 동양 철학을 적용하여 3가지 요소 간의 조화를 구현하고 더 많은 모음을 개발했단다." 엄마가 말해요.

"And these three basic shapes were combined to create the first six vowels, ㅏ (ah), ㅓ (eo), ㅗ(o), ㅜ(oo), ㅡ(eu), ㅣ(ee), and double vowels were created by adding another horizontal or vertical stroke, ㅑ (ya), ㅕ (yeo), ㅘ(wah), ㅛ(yo), ㅞ(weh), ㅠ (yu)." Mom says.

"그리고 이 세 가지 기본 모양이 결합되어 첫 여섯 개의 모음이 만들어졌어, 아, 어, 오, 우, 으, 이, 그리고 이중모음은 다른 가로 또는 세로 획을 추가해서 만들어졌지, 야, 여, 와, 요, 웨, 유." 엄마가 말해요.

"It is really impressive how these letters were created based on the universe." Emily says with admiration. Mom tells Emily that Hangeul was first officially adopted in 1894 with widespread effects to promote its goodness, however there were incidents that prohibited the use of the Korean language, such as during the Japanese colonial period.

"이 문자가 우주를 기반으로 만들어졌다는 게 정말 인상적이에요." 에밀리가 감탄하며 말해요. 엄마는 에밀리에게 한글이 1894년에 처음 공식적으로 채택되어 그 장점을 널리 알리는데 큰 영향을 미쳤지만, 일제 강점기 동안에 한국어 사용을 금지한 사건들도 있었다고 말씀 하세요.

Mom goes on. "Then with the end of the occupation in 1945, Korean was re-established as the official language and so we are able to use the wonderful Hangeul today."

엄마가 계속 말해요. "그러다가 1945년 점령이 끝나면서 한국어가 공식 언어로 다시 확립 되었고 그래서 우리가 오늘날 훌륭한 한글을 사용할 수 있게 되었지."

"Korean people also celebrate Hangeul day." Mom says. "Oh, really?" Emily is surprised with the fact. "It's annually on October 9th to show appreciation for King Sejong's creativity and honouring the excellence of Hangeul, it was registered with UNESCO in 1997 as well. Its inclusion recognizes Hangeul as a scientific and important piece of cultural heritage." Mom states.

"한국인들은 또한 한글날을 기념하기도 해." 엄마가 말해요. "아, 정말요?" 에밀리는 그 사실에 놀라워 해요. "매년 10월 9일은 세종대왕의 창의성에 감사를 표하고 한글의 우수성을 기리기 위한 날이지, 1997년에는 유네스코에도 등록이 되었단다. 그건 한글을 과학적이고 중요한 문화유산으로 인정한다는 걸 의미해." 엄마가 이야기 해요.

"That is wonderful!" Emily cheers proudly. Mom shows her the basic shape of syllables in Korean which are consonant+vowel, for example '가'(ga) or consonant+vowel+consonant, like the word 강(gang). She lets Emily know Korean letters are written like building a house.

"정말 멋져요!" 에밀리가 자랑스럽게 외쳐요. 엄마는 에밀리에게 한국어 음절의 기본 형태인 자음+모음, 예를 들어 '가', 또는 자음+모음+자음 으로된 '강' 같은 단어를 보여주죠. 한국어 글자가 집을 짓는 것 처럼 쓰여진 다는 것도 알려주어요.

"I think I can write Hangeul now." Emily announces confidently. "H pronounces ㅎ, a pronounces ㅏ and n pronounces ㄴ." Emily accomplishes the first letter and concentrates for the second one. "And g pronounces ㄱ, eu pronounces ㅡ and l pronounces ㄹ."

"이제 한글을 쓸 수 있을 것 같아요." 에밀리가 자신 있게 말 해요. "H는 ㅎ으로 발음하고, a는 ㅏ로 발음하고 n은 ㄴ으로 발음해요." 에밀리가 첫 글자를 완성하고 두 번째 글자에 집중해요. "그리고 g는 ㄱ으로 발음하고, eu는 ㅡ로 그리고 l은 ㄹ으로 발음해요."

She completes it slowly but clearly 한글. The horizontal, vertical and circle are all harmonized magically. She is delighted. "That is so neat." Mom lovingly embraces her. Now Emily knows more about Korean song lyrics. She cherishes Korean music even more as she recalls the joy of learning Korean.

에밀리는 천천히 그러나 분명하게 한글을 완성해요. 수평, 수직 그리고 원이 모두 마법처럼 조화를 이루어요. 에밀리가 기뻐하죠. "멋지게 잘 썼구나." 엄마가 에밀리를 다정하게 안아주어요. 이제 에밀리는 한국어 노래 가사에 대해 더 많이 알게 되었어요. 한국어를 배우는 즐거움을 떠올리면서 한국음악을 더욱 소중히 여기게 되었죠.

Emily already imagines asking for directions and ordering food in Korean. She would love to learn about other captivating Korean traditions too. Knowing and understanding new words make her feel different. She really looks forward to the day she can speak this beautiful language freely. It will lead to many adventures.

에밀리는 이미 길을 묻고 음식을 주문하는 것을 한국어로 상상하고 있어요. 다른 아주 멋진 한국 전통에 대해서도 배우고 싶어하죠. 새로운 단어를 알고 이해한다는 건 기분을 다르게 느끼게 만들어요. 에밀리는 이 아름다운 언어를 자유롭게 말할 수 있는 날을 정말로 고대하고 있어요. 그것은 많은 모험으로 이끌어 줄거에요.

20 Basic Korean Sentences

Sentence & Romanization	Translation
1. 안녕하세요 [an nyeong ha se yo]	hello
2. 잘 지냈어요? [jal ji nae sso yo]	how have you been?
3. 안녕히 가세요 [an nyeong hi ga se yo]	goodbye
4. 좋은 하루 보내세요 [jo eun ha ru bo nae se yo]	have a nice day
5. 감사합니다 [gam sa ham ni da]	thank you
6. 죄송합니다 [joe song ham ni da]	I'm sorry
7. 제 이름은... 입니다 [je i reum eun ... im ni da]	my name is ...
8. 괜찮아요 [gwaen chan a yo]	I'm ok, it's ok
9. 천천히 말해 주세요 [cheon cheon hi mal hae ju se yo]	please, speak slowly
10. 지금 뭐 해요 [ji geum mwo hae yo]	what are you doing now
11. 추워요 [chu weo yo]	it's cold
12. 더워요 [deo weo yo]	it's hot
13. 이해해요 [i hae hae yo]	I understand
14. 잘 자요 [jal ja yo]	sleep well
15. 집에 가요 [jib e ga yo]	I'm going home
16. 좋아요 [jo a yo]	it's nice / good
17. 싫어요 [sil eo yo]	I don't like it
18. 알겠어요 [al get seo yo]	I got it
19. 모르겠어요 [mo reu get seo yo]	I don't know
20. 생일 축하해요 [saeng il chuk ha hae yo]	happy birthday

Korean Consonant Practice

ㄱ												
ㄴ												
ㄷ												
ㄹ												
ㅁ												
ㅂ												
ㅅ												
ㅇ												
ㅈ												
ㅊ												
ㅋ												
ㅌ												
ㅍ												
ㅎ												

Korean Vowel Practice

ㅏ						
ㅑ						
ㅓ						
ㅕ						
ㅗ						
ㅛ						
ㅜ						
ㅠ						
ㅡ						
ㅣ						

Korean Alphabet Practice

	ㅏ	ㅑ	ㅓ	ㅕ	ㅗ	ㅛ	ㅜ	ㅠ	ㅡ	ㅣ
ㄱ										
ㄴ										
ㄷ										
ㄹ										
ㅁ										
ㅂ										
ㅅ										
ㅇ										
ㅈ										
ㅊ										
ㅋ										
ㅌ										
ㅍ										
ㅎ										

Korean Alphabet Practice Sheet

Her passion extends to various art forms. She especially loves all the simple and pure images of nature and has been writing and illustrating children's book for more than 10 years. She was born in Korea and moved to Canada in 2001 and lives with her husband and daughter in Toronto.

More books by Seong min Yoo

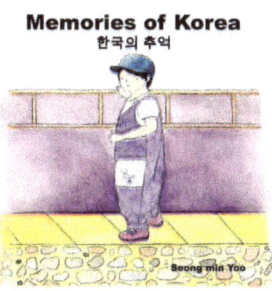
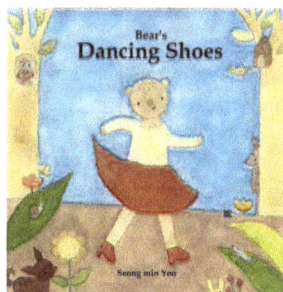

www.ingramcontent.com/pod-product-compliance
Lightning Source LLC
Chambersburg PA
CBHW061151070526
44584CB00034B/4482